gone

gone

all gone

poems by Andrew Condouris

gone, gone, all gone
Copyright ©2022 Andrew Condouris
Cover Art- "Sora" Oleg Onchky

ISBN-

Published by:

Blue Jade Press, LLC

Blue Jade Press, LLC
Vineland, NJ 08360
www.bluejadepress.com

This collection would not be possible without the help of many people. First, my Thursday Bunch Writing Group in Princeton. Thanks to Karen Chaffee, Diana Ferry, Jessie Krause, and Jennifer Tobin.

I would also like to give my heartfelt thanks to Eric Maywar at Classics Bookstore in Trenton for giving me a place to start over again.

Extra special thanks to Todd Evans for showing me anything is possible.

To my wife, Rachel

TABLE OF CONTENTS

CHRONICLE

Before the moment of birth I was pushing
against the walls to make my fingerprints
the more I tried to know the world's face
the more it knew mine funny how that works
or maybe not so funny nowadays

I'm born into the past at least I think
I was the snowstorm bristling
across town supposedly I'm not sure

not the best witness am I? the public records
account for me the weather and the roving stars
aligned or otherwise it's all been filed

except the roaring swashes dark and light
and for all I know the midwife tripped
on something nearly broke her stethoscope
my father and my mother out-and-out
wouldn't remember such a detail birth
rings seismic even mine the particulars fall

into the bell of a screaming mouth
of course my mother ensured me my arrival
was something graceful and ethereal

   you purred as softly as a newborn kitten
   no drama or complications no bad news

of course the bad news comes later
like when you go from everything's aware
to who am I this time? A donkey starving stuck
between two bales of hay or when you see

1

this business of life is a thing that happens
to you

sometimes more than once

all I know is that we are born in a car crash
completely helpless each begging to come home
I'm still not sure what we're supposed to do

I'm still not sure what I'm supposed to do

       look this cloud ushers light across
       the sky return the dark return to me
       return

GASLIGHTS

Of thee and other flames I rhyme
again your dim lights hid
the crimes of wealth the balanced
books gargantuan and blood-black your faint
light let the shadows gather
'round circumference tighten
red handprints fade perhaps they winged
into the linden trees in such an ink
I made up constellations
safe in my derision quiet convulsions
of a smile I flew like that
for years pretending to sleep
like a sacred cow in the lion's den
how long before I'd allow
the gift of foolishness? laughing
at a broken toy the fireflies are glowing
the summer's breathing

some monsters wait
till dark descends

VIOLIN

The bow flies up then hangs aloft
the quiver just before you start the piece
heart wants heat heat wants heart's industry
my stomach sparkles in the dark a gem of glory
glory fingers tapping secrets the floorboards
creaking silky silence out I roll my program
into a telescope to find the constellation Doubt
your bow descends like a falcon to the kill

and now I'm back at the bottom of the sea
a diver who begs the shimmering dark to light
the way to the end of all of his meddling
a diver who loves his weights a bit too much
I see a Stranger sleepwalking home
her purple swirls adrift — Anemone tell
my restless mind the reason we caress
or else caress caress it's for the best
divine what's variation and anomaly please
for I can't speak myself into history
only what is wriggling writhing and squirming
will dance these ancient currents into relief
make space and time the darlings of my blood

the Stranger speaks: I know it would be great
to have a hand reach out and hold yours tight
and carry you into the black the raptures
of the deep your head aglow doom-tongues
no longer licking all about your face
it'd be great too if I had hands to give
instead take solace since the sea is Yes
and thank you all are welcome in my arms
there's nothing wrong with drifting peacefully

4

into dark heaven fat underbelly of moonlight—
beauty's there and for the first time in a long time
you needn't look away

a bubble rises up before me heading
for The King of Shadows I am surprised
to follow—though in my own time and now
I'm one pure thing a bubble in the flux
I know what I am doing—I am Sense

you slowly lift the bow away
I lost your song by digging for it here
in the bosom of a rotten mind unraveling
with loss and rank derision I should steal
the goddamn thing I'll wait outside your door
and steal your instrument this thing of joy
will show me what I missed I'll shake it out

         or else Anemone was the song I heard

I never see it as it is a breath receiving
another breath an ocean yields unto the stars
reflections of a dream and I attend
the masters in between

PIG

Now students if you cannot do the work
because religion plays a role because
the pigs are taken from the mother's womb
when she is slaughtered well you'll get a C

the teacher had a secret face a snarl
suppressed beneath her lips her oval glasses
withdrew the spark from pea-green eyes
when she handed out the babes we had a hunch
she'd birthed them from herself with hands
beneath her skirt she lured them out
with formaldehyde too

we placed our dozing baby in the tray
her little tongue poked out for your warm milk
the fine hairs of her legs betrayed an ache
we could not name you opened her with a razor
made flaps of skin like children's hands in prayer
removed her rib cage she would reveal
her soft secrets made of gold and pearls

beheld the grey-gone heart & lungs of her
and what was once an impish light was engulfed
by dark as she split open broke
apart from eons past and eons hence

And in the breaking the darkness spreads
the whoring of our love and what for all this rack
did we receive? for all her pain and ours

we got a B

CHERRY-FLAVORED

I was your third boy you were my first
and in the church our kisses flared

towered high as angels and warmed
the vault in the pews we blundered

over each other me clumsy with a tug
on your tie and vest and skirt as I held

you closer diving into mouths and mouths
of your fevered blood while you grabbed

the sharp starchy creases of my pants
our black shoes squeaked your lipstick

poured heat on my tongue and spread
I was your third boy you were my first kiss

and God was the imprint of the cushion
on your cheek lingering in force

and then fearing holiness up and fled
the church to hear and see the first buds

of spring ache into existence

SMALL TALK

Discuss doors objects but have a limit
of how many objects about which you are willing
to make conversation say twenty don't be the nut
who discusses things until they disappear discuss
literature perhaps or proper safety when repairing

a garage door all things are of mucho significance
at all times or discuss tea or how cats always land
on their paws not a miraculous event yet wow
the world is so large and so small and so on
everything contains everything else discuss dogs

really get down to brass tacks about dogs
because no one else is gonna dredge up
the hard-cold truth think it through or yawn
speak on behalf of the permanence of things speak
of industrious elbows jabbing through the mire

towards the climes of plastic tomorrows or speak
truly about true things the beginning of a disease
a forest fire a dream of stolen horses the purple hills
closing in on the dam a mouth opening in the dead
of night the souls of rabbits the thousand cardboard

boxes of your life the vanishing saint
speak plainly and without distortion speak
of that work party around Christmas when you fell
asleep drunk on a pile of winter coats
in the bedroom in the dark with the blue chatter

rattling around the house someone came kissed
you on the cheek and talk about how you woke up

a few seconds later still in darkness you wandered
around the house in a daze whispering to shrinking
co-workers to figure out who planted that kiss

on you you still wonder your heart goes light
as ashes cross the sky would it help if I said
it was me? o please speak! elaborate talk up
the idiocy of spinning satellites how everything
is too much/not enough how it's all out of joint

time space and gravity and all that too besides
okay maybe don't bring all of that up maybe stick
to the rumors and gossip of the week and the turn
of the wind in whichever direction it so chooses
and the stock market stick to the script

at least this time around

COMEDIAN

No speaking today I'll let my throat rest
there there I know I deserve a moment's peace
from the noise the jabbering I deserve a day
alone with my voice the audience can wait
give me a cigarette

you know something's been troubling me
as of late my voice is twisting to sound
like yours not that yours is all that grating
or bad even I just prefer my voice to yours
pass me those matches

it's been a long year but my suffering's small
kittens eating butterflies a cigarette heals
this hunt in the skin the silence is forgotten
whoosh now we know everything exploded
in a quiet orderly fashion

some nights I dream of simpler times than these
those days of anonymity those days I'd walk
the streets and shine my face to whoever saw it

some nights I hear the hurdy-gurdy soul approach
my bed she slips beneath the covers holds me close
curls her wings around me

my throat

TELEPHONE

Sometimes our heart goes square
a room below the sea fluorescent lights
acoustic tile a table chairs an empty room
a rotary phone on the floor ringing
like it's Judgement Day all brassy
and who will answer it?

the bells are bouncing
all around the room
like some agreement's struck
the sky forgets the sea
the birds forget the earth the waves
forget the moon the kiss
this system of exchange

the ringing rings for us silent bugbears
o hellions who thirst for what is true
let ring the chimes steer the spinning
dial home you transform augment

this song is lifting us calling us near
it calls down the stars too for we live
nowhere now what once was doom
is now the salty blood of second chances
hear the ring of bells of gongs bending
the corners and say no more for us
they ring unto eternity

SIREN

You're drunk your hand is flapping lazily
your long unruly hair's so lush it bleeds
you're lying naked cigarette in hand
imbibing whiskey watching *The Price is Right*
your eyes don't leave the TV not once
contestants spin the wheel and pray for love

your legs at the end of the unmade bed
the empty cans and bottles the ashtrays
filled to the brim with cigarettes condoms
on the floor odd stains and everywhere
empty cartons of take-out food you stamp
your cigarette out and clear your throat

      I gotta go back to work
      can you carry me?

you put your arms out I come to your side
and pick you up cradle you in my arms

      you're such the gentleman
      you whisper

I carry you out of the room & across the lot
towards the bright boom of the noonday waves
I walk us into the sea the water so cold
shooting bolts of ice up my legs

you kiss my nose then swirl with mastery
into the murk you make a leap in the spindrift
you're a thing now with razor-sharp teeth
glistening wild with blue then you're gone

12

a gull cries out
        return to us
        the sailors have grown
        too bold we're begging you
        please return ensnare them
        with your voice

I walk back to the motel in the rain
grateful for the ground beneath my feet

ENTERING THE CITY AT DAWN

The moon she spins and falls
the guests run away
from your soiree your house
crushes into diamonds
the sun threatens to march
through these fated woods

we lovers go henceforth
to Manhattan to reclaim
the spirit of prophecy I run
red lights tires grip whispers
skip you record my dreams
on 16mm my skull of smog

I slice straight through
macadam and river-mouth waves
of traffic doubling trebling
the day moon stops to watch
the sunlight flashing through
windows in a 3/4 waltz

you keep your Bolex clicking
dreams stick to silver I see myself
in the black and white grind of
due consideration we end
where the harbor swells

we speak of our times apart
the birth of our fables
the psychic year is ours to burn
——or the negative

you drive us
across the bridge
your mouth moving
with no sound

the day consumes us

ACCIDENT

Youth is brighter than death and invincibly lost
invincibly dumb beneath the old owls crossing
the reservoir at night see us snake up and down
the hills in the little black Nissan fleeing heaven
with radio cutting "Over the Hills and Far Away"
into polkas and sports announcers and color-dead
static and Yes our own screaming as we rocket
through the rails the reservoir fence down and up
into the thick of the woods around Newark's water
supply the police come the ambulance the fire truck

        you idiots are lucky to be alive
                a fireman says
        only last week a truck driver flew off
        the same spot and a fence post run him
        through the heart

sometimes I close my eyes and they open
into a secret story a videotape I see the belly
of the little black Nissan ripped wide open
by the fence pole see the guts snake and split
everything pops out a sneeze the vivisection
of rainbows tentacles and sores and a viscous
liquid gunking up the works scratch marks
where the branches tried to fight brain matter
of the transmission no curves nothing changes
even if history's shook up and all the pieces
rearranged headlights blinking eyes looking out
into the void of their own declarations tires soft
as dewy grass the treads unicursal labyrinths

when the headlights flashed into the trees
they held up their branches like old hands
holding back fate the womb of the night
held us told us we were gods in Jell-o
forever held in some psychotic's wish
laughing we were laughing as we flew
into the end tied to nothing an assumption
of infinite lives an insult to civilization
our laughter fusing in the air

brighter and bigger than death
is youth but invincibly small
an ember in the dark woods
so far from the purring stars
an ember waiting for the wind
to kiss it awake

OCTOPUS

I turn on the TV hear the chatter and buzz
of the news consonants and vowels crackle
I'm looking for the news you're okay

I look in the mirror eight days since I shaved
evident insomnia my face is scattershot some bit
of dream left in my eyes a plumb line dragging up
gods from the deep reach

from my iris a swirling bother a fleck a drop of ink
rises in the air towards the ceiling blotting
in a dumbshow of weird what the sun draws
into trees and rocks and abandoned works

      the blue ink spreads

an octopus unwinds her arms black maw emerges
in her world of eight known paths every wish
somewhere between my wits floating in ether
suspended my head fills with bicycle bells clicking
crosswalks edge of the room stretches contracts
ah grace is not everything octopus descends sinks
suckers expanding gripping at a slight crack
in the wall moving spider-like a tender grasp
on the molding firm grip on the dresser-top taking
me into her vise ticklish blessed arms running
swiftly down my spine her beak snaps open
my jaw she scuttles down my throat
curse upon curse finds no air

THE WIRES

I am what the river wants tonight
wildflowers grow a dream to dream away
I remember an atom quark a friction
you left me cut and bruised as sky
now I speak into the dark looking over
my shoulders for this wandering love adrift
in your old gardens adrift in heartache lost
as Salome inside the Baptist's mouth

      the river speaks

you spent your best days and nights in search
of where the wires end and that's a crime
you looked so hard for answers you forgot
the questions well that's alright don't you fret
I'll make it so you don't forget it's hard to make
the river cry yet still it happens by and by

you will arise from up my drink and walk
into the heart of certainties and don't forget
your kettle of fish you're welcome

TIGERS

You draw your asymmetric tigers
over and over and I sit and smile inside
because we are not ready to smile
on the outside not till they adjust our doses

when you look up at me I want to say
it's not madness running your fever
and there is nothing in your hands
but your hands

I oughta tell myself that first
and I should tell myself the substance
of light is not darkness and no thieves
want the jewels from my head

and function does follow form but leave
it to the experts in your dream of tigers
there are no flaws despite what humans say

what about this one? I ask

      you say
      she is the one who flashed
      in the waving grass
      who said virtue began in vice
      who held your hand and led you
      here to the jungle

and here in the jungle I do not question
the trembling leaves or the voice
in the canopy or question to whom
this heat belongs these curls of fever
turn the evening red amber eyes
circle ever in the shadows behind me

EXILE OF DAEDALUS

Beneath a ruck of stars the pulsing waves
sustain me as I surrender to the whims
of wind and moon here lost beneath the eye
embracing the sea I make the sum of me

an architect who built on drifting clouds
inventor of his own entropic storms
a man who couldn't smell the past or present
so focused on the future's vague design

the moonlight curls its arms under my arms
I rise to meet my end at last waves oscillate

but how can I rise when just one wave
might bring me back to you?

the boat embraces land

       kiss kiss kiss
       o silly me silly engineer

it's death to entrust
my end upon the spheres

       alight alight

JOB INTERVIEW

It's raining small steel nails the taste
gets on my tongue I want to see my face
my suit my least-wrinkled tie boots
as yellow as bananas ripe for cutting
up ahead an umbrella expands
Renoir's ol' *Boating Party* the rain sneaks
down my collar

I want to be a hammer pounding
those nails of purpose building love
or some entirely reasonable substitute
I'm done with counting birds on a branch
I know our spaceship's crashed on Jupiter
perhaps no one's coming for us

> I have to get this job
> be somebody other
> than love's plaything

as the email instructed
I enter the building take the elevator
in steel and glass gravity arrives at long last
away we go high above the river bridge above
attic dreams above the phases of the moon
above the broken heart the roller coaster
those twenty open mouths

up here my eyes are empty as the night
you returned a black witch moth bleeding
in your palms I knew it then the wheel breaks
when I awake in the natural order of things
awake and float in milk float

23

the interview is cancelled last minute
the guy who's supposed to go after me
his interview is cancelled too his voice
is a child's sketch of the sun but something
comes from nothing he leaves his umbrella
Renoir's ol' *Boating Party* the elevator sinks
to the Earth I step outside open Renoir
rain falls those silver nails they calculate
upon the *Party* I am lost adrift in heaven
with no compass or map

find me
wherever you are find me

RED-WINGED BLACKBIRD

And here you come again a leap
another then skittering flash
across the muddy puddles your beak adorned
with dripping gore I know it's you
the one who stayed in my attic last winter
after the blizzards killed
my trees you were a decent tenant
kept to yourself

and I know it's you who danced
the Charleston around the wires
after last night's cloudburst
your morning song for stranger days
you seemed to dance
for sweet oblivion as though it were
the missing ingredient

do you remember me?

I'm the one who stood there
all week long at the fork in the path awaiting
your answer your yearning cry what simmers
in my blood

I'm your closest stranger your compatriot
of middle distances effortlessly

you gave the breath of life
your cries gave me heaven heaven
the black hole heart of galaxies
heaven

WILD HORSES

The horses run
on bloated bellies
along the surf
their foals run astride
such wobbling legs
deserve the earth
a thousand miles
south-southwest

with hooves
in shallows
losing sun
dark laughter
smacking through
the waves their spirits
drive the spirits
straight into the heart
of our unreason

a black sun rises
over these wilds
its light reveals
the wisps of us
our curve's refusal
to admit the terminal
nature of love

when horses horse
I know our love
when grasses take
the breeze I know
the hand holding

the hand
holding
the light
the dark
the promise

BOOKS

It's this thing I used to do when I was a child
run my fingers over the titles of the books
taking one down and flipping through trying
to find myself in the pages but I was stuck
I couldn't see how the ocean of words
decided to be fantastic how the bravest thing
they could do was be extraordinarily ordinary
like picking up cigarette butts off the porch
like listening to a bee as it made its way
around my room

I did not yet know everything loses
its meaning even the numbers stuck with faith
and if you're lucky you see past the end
of divinity you see your girlfriend running
her hand along the spines pulling out
a thin book finding that #9 poem in *Pictures
From a Gone World* by Lawrence Ferlinghetti

> "but then finally one day / she who has always
> been so timid / offs with her glove and says /
> (though not in so many big words) Let's lie down
> somewheres / baby"

SHARKS

The door is open wide I don't remember
locking it perhaps the wind? or someone
broke in

well

to call the police involves a later bedtime
sleep is all I crave these days I guess I'll walk
around the manse a couple of times and check
the nooks and crannies all the hiding places
once upon a time when he would disappear
behind the boxes never emptied
not even after the basement flooded
I just bought new ones

what are boxes when filled with junk
you can't remember? walls or prisons or mazes
or a secret tunnel leading us to all the sharks
this fragile planet holds

how angry was I? well your head explodes
until it doesn't right? so many sharks ruined
concrete to me yet I kept up the jig
such love could feel the grooves forming
the dusky shark the hammerhead the white
the sandbar shark the spiny dogfish

all of them swimming where black waves flow
no pause or doubt no hidden cameras peeping
just a silvery and awful grace twisting
into the murk and she might leave
her crimson tracks in the dawn

a bigger maze to solve the bourbon bloom
of wish and rage after he was gone I would
not admit the hollowing dark rising I still
swim in it I really do believe he's here now
hiding about to jump out

boo!

he still walks ten feet in front
and behind me asking strangers
if they're his Ma running back to me
with questions about the impossible sun

the house is empty more empty
than it's ever been I turn the lights on
for the spirits here right now

there's only one thief in this house
he's stealing from the past to avoid
this moment he's going to get caught
someday

NOTES FOR A FILM

Remember the audience is blind
don't talk about what's invisible don't hint

the eroticism of a light switch? nuh-uh
also the characters must enjoy empty space
and no one fits there more than the criminal
have someone say

> money was invented
> so we don't have to look each other
> in the eyes

or something to that effect just tell the truth
but not your truth end with animals killing
each other or with a stretch of trees
and a winding road a black car rolling up
branches waving back and forth nothing
but circles inside the circles ankles twisting
forgetting black car rolling bug floating
around inside strange-looking thing a beetle
or a moth fat with wings you can't see slips
into your mouth you swallow the whole thing
in one gulp

maybe it's for the best

REPLY

Got your email yesterday I can't sleep
either the nights expand or contract
and sometimes I hear my brainwaves
all in all I am doing okay I take it slow

the desert air heals
not in some wishy-washy way
something here takes
over your soul even so I miss
all the songs back home tell Harry

I said hello tell her I am
all right the desert life the quiet
and the new companionship's done me well
I am stripped of all my impurities

of all things untrue I am growing young
soon I will be inside the womb of the sun soon
I will be inside the fire no more suits of light
no more desperation no waiting for her plane

to land spotting her amongst arrivals I'm sorry
by the way for taking her love away from you
you made it so easy Mama always said to leave
folks happier than how I found them

which is how I knew I had to leave
one more way to ease her mind

I still tell jokes sometimes but I don't joke
for just anyone anymore no sir I've opened
my windows to let in the wind and sorrow

the comings and goings of our mutual owls
the crooked fingers cannot point I've gone
astray into the hollow sun and tumbled down
into the ditch another lonely child of the earth

who won't yield to honeybells or crows falling
at his naked feet the stones have chosen me
the low hills have chosen me I have found

in their bends the echoes of the hunters
of eternal nights of white wheels spinning out

anyhow I hope Harry is dreaming
I hope you have forgiveness in your heart
for the one who couldn't move
an inch without blowing up the works

in another life we are co-workers running
into each other downtown in another life
we are throwing aces onto the tracks
but I am working on being alone

(in wild dreams I come to my deathbed scene
a warm hand in mine a suspicion of lilacs violets
lilies you're not there and that's fine)

alone—even with my new companions how long
does it take to get alone in this world?

come visit and discover for yourself

IN PRAISE OF

Your tiny voice will be heard
above the din you needn't levitate
or perform magic tricks unless you prefer to

people remember people like us
people who circle the wide zeroes no king
dreamt you up you are as real as me sure
there are folks who jump

off bridges and there's those who catch them
don't make yourself sick trying to figure out
who is who just remember

the gooseflesh and pearls the garden
will be finished and the flowers will be watered
the way they should be mail will pile up

mostly because I will keep writing you
in my chicken scratches just remember
you're carried by under-dreams

by gods cracking foxy
everything is going to be okay even if it's not
especially if it's not for the Earth must spin
and the Moon must plot

SHOPPING CART

It is a thing I fill a-brim
with lots of crap organic and processed
fleshy and frosty ice cream and hot sauce
share a space as I toss my shit into the belly
of the cage a hollow voice rattles off
the specials on the PA a voice losing color
talks to the ghosts amongst the pears I bop
through the cereal aisle with grit and verve
faces asking for whom would he descend
into hell?

when I get outside the snowstorm
sings and dances so I abandon my cart
near my car it's such a sad sight to see

this vessel this womb that's fed me
so well left behind in the blindness
left alone to wait for mercy wait for time
to send it crawling back to the ocean
to the goo of variables the place where
finally the universe loves us
because we are not here

CONNECTING FLIGHT

My bones sustain me I count on my fingers
these eight hours

sleep chases me across the night golden jaws snap
in my face

once upon a time I had one string attached
to everything but now

the knot rises from my belly in jabs and juts
and explodes my mouth with webs and nets

they avoid me on the plane in all the terminals
they know I'm gone across to the other shore

not all destinations are known minds open a trick
of the sun

aren't we funny feeling for a face in the dark?
searching for someone to wear this crown of stars?

MALMÖ

The busker sings her songs guitar circling a falling
chord it's enough for me the dude who sleeps
at operas and awakes on the empty stage to find
everybody's gone home it is enough for me falling
backward into the arctic night the sun goes
down with the busker's voice an orange escapes
her bag and rolls around the pavement I stop
the orange with my foot its tenderness is real

I pick it up

       my aches are mine and all these scars
       belong to me all I can carry all I can hold

I place the orange in her shaking hands

COPENHAGEN

Against myself against the numbing nights I want
now to belong I take the train to town and hit
a coffeehouse where jazz pleases the posing punks
and I the idiot writer writing screenplays sick
with negative capability fall into the spaces the
notes the jabs and blares evening transposes
us into our true configurations the magic hides
in songs within the songs

we smoke and drink and speak of lovers
how they save the moon and yes we know
who invited the lion who asked the sun
to rise we carry ourselves in swarms
in consciousness alone the darkness swims
fantasies of milk and honey o is my mouth
still moving? I'm sorry if I'm screaming
I thought I was whispering

see my mind is failing me it was failing
me before I was born and it will forget
me after I am gone

but look at the heart holding it up to stars
it beats with dreams of summers in Spain
of the cool in comet's tails always milk
always honey and the hour owns itself
again again again one less tear
for Lazarus

HOUSE

The hurricane comes late at night but we're all safe
warm Sophia's on the couch teaching us the rules
of the game by candlelight while the wind and snow
and sleet rage overhead

and I think of good old Don Quixote tipping
at the three windmills outside the rain and snow
and sleet sinking into his bones his poor horse
sticking by his side a faithful servant to the end
and Panza lost

in faithfulness someone brings Sophia reindeer tea
water and bread for the rest of us

I watch the windmills' blinking lights
through the watery windows and the cypresses
dancing on the property line as the sleet falls
sideways Sophia throws in three more logs warms
her hands by the fire and listens to the wind

                    she speaks

when I was a child I wanted to save the world
but I forgot I was part of it I forgot love
and laughter are my birthrights instead I was
a dreamer who forgot she was dreaming

but now I am awake and I will awaken
you as well you will become soldiers protecting
my falling starseed you will become the cloud
leave your toys you will live as children
of the revolution growing higher

than the sun you will tear down
the House of Man & rebuild your soul
all your pieces fell into other people
long ago

look around
we each carry a piece of you

let us begin the work
of gathering you up

BLUE FUNK

I wake up in a red wooden chair
the blue walls surround me I rise then fall
next to the shower drain
behind the chair the door darker blue tense I crawl
over and try the knob locked I can't hear
anything outside just my breathing the floating
stones in my head come out of my mouth and build
a pyramid with each stone I lose
myself the pyramid grows
higher and higher the stones crack
and the shards catch
the sunlight

Z

Everything is still the storm has passed
three feet of snow out there Åke won't be back
anytime soon

the house creaks and groans
of an eternal return an old house well-used
the foundation is the only thing remaining
from the original construction Åke told me

he left
two days ago went to work up north
installing windows I dream
the house is taken apart bit by bit
and rebuilt elsewhere—that house will be
the same house

I'm not too fond
of questions but they come up when the snow
and attendant silence won't stop I start to question
everything when the storm howled
I knew was enslaved
to my senses but now with the sun
in the tree line there's a deeper more fretful
darkness some creeping thing

I found a camcorder in the closet
it actually fell on my head while I was reaching
to get a pair of wool gloves off the shelf

there was only one tape
the one marked 'Z' inside of the machine
the machine was dead but I found

the charger in the desk upstairs

It's Åke ten years younger a voice full of vim
and vigor he's just found out he is going to be
a father the cheerfulness is rather ironic considering
the path his life will take

how Z slips
through his fingers in the courtroom the surgical
dance of parents ripped
from their children's lives forever

I think about throwing
the tape into the fireplace I return
it to its place in the machine and then I place
the machine in the closet exactly where I found
it on the shelf

when Åke returns
I won't tell him what I found
I'll let him stumble
across it in his own due time

The house creaks and groans in the morning light
I spend the day reading Ulysses I lose my focus
and concentration quite easily the book is dying
and yet it seems to go on and on trying to make
its point something to do with time who cares?
I shouldn't have to do all the work across the vast
expanse between writer and reader I ask him to give
me the short version

no reply the house creaks and groans
Åke returns by nightfall

NAVIGATING YOUR WAY INTO A
SAINT'S EAR

The saint is approachable now he's eaten
his fill of the pastrami sandwich he's drunk
four beers in the space of an hour I whisper
into his ear tell him I'm paying our rent
with my blood it's a lot of blood and I notice

I become someone else when I am eating
a cookie but blood isn't enough I whisper
into his ear about the hands I held
about the tongues in my mouth see the knots
and curves and cankers reaching
into my yesterdays the saint mumbles
back to me from his sleep

        you know better than to interrupt my
        post-lunch naps

his bright planet acts in accordance
with his 574 moons his scales tip
back and forth into desire the rest of us give
our blood eat our cookies and float
toward something vaguely resembling heaven

FROM THE DREAMHOUSE

help me to recall
looking everywhere for ah-ha should've
been looking for uh-huh we heard horses
last night I think they were zebras
protect me from me keep
me in my reveries keep me from the windows
say there are ghosts in the walls revelations
between the stones come off the roof come
down from spider dreams come find
me in my room I'm writing on the water
eating up the long shadows

come close I'm playing the piano for you I'm
wrestling with the angel of memory too much
of a good thing took us halfway there the stars
are still boiling in the basement
the boilerman keeps this machine blazing
and bubbling and his records show the hour
when coming and going started to look
the same when he sees us he sees
we are children interrupting
the adults in the middle of a conversation

come off the roof we don't have to save
the world let's watch a black and white movie
and laugh our mothers will protect us
shut our mouths with a wave
from the dream house

CROUCHING CAT

A bird flitters
in its nest I wait for it to fly
down from the shreds of carpet and snips
of wood and metal now it is pecking
at the dirt and I only approach
while it is eating
so it does not hear me I pounce
and take its life
the planets are orbiting
the Sun
the gods are nowhere
I float the sky is blue
then a darker blue then stars the humans
are nowhere but that's nothing new
I can see Mars shining
I have always been traveling
in space silence is nothing new
later I will return
and kill another bird
but we are approaching
infinity now

DEBT

I cannot remember
to whom I've agreed to an experiment in any case
I report to the office every morning at 9 am
and watch TV until 5 pm I am entertained
without the use of advertising

       hit the happier button when happier
       and the sadder button when sadder

on the TV a woman is telling a man she loves
him he doesn't love her but he loves the idea of her
ok whatever I change the channel and find a show
about bread making I change the channel
and I am given instructions on how to survive
on Planet Earth including where one should live
depending on whether they're cold-blooded
or warm-blooded the hard and fast rules
for the animal kingdom such as kill or be killed
and survival of the ones most likely to reproduce
I change the channel and learn

notation for a C major scale
the runic alphabet numbers zero through 10
and I write down two plus two equals five
I want to rediscover our species or how to peel
a banana how to tell a joke how to pack
a suitcase for a weekend trip how to shampoo
your locks how to tell a white lie I change
the channel again to see a woman walking
down a long hallway it's the hallway outside
my door she stops in front of my door of course
and knocks

the hand in the circle leaves
no trace who holds
your hand?

ah she's The Lady Who Eats Spiders she gets me
confused sometimes an itch a pang an urge to walk
around the block what makes the night pulsate
and jump but I know enough not to ask her
who I am

a spider
spinning my web

PIANO PLAYER

I try to play but my left hand refuses
the stroke did me in I won't pretend
otherwise no one knows I come here
daily to see what I can do my last concert
was the first time I felt God move my hands
and then He went and cooked my brain

83 years old if I have any grudge
couldn't He just paralyze my left leg instead?
why's He have to make an example out of
an idiot from Paterson New Jersey I sit and pour
another drink fumbling with the bottle

I go and sit where the ghost
was sitting on the couch place the little mirror
next to the notebook no one recognizes me
no one recognizes me because I'm so old
no that's not true I'm still stopped
in the streets these days by photographers
or fans asking for autographs

I pick up my pen and continue writing my notes
I keep my left hand behind the mirror
I look over every few seconds to see the illusion
in the mirror of my left hand dancing
across the notebook with the pen as though the
stroke never happened as though I am writing
two memoirs two lessons in what not to do
if you want people to love and to love you

the left hand moves like a ballerina another ghost
another dead day I write all the things I've heard
from other musicians over the years

> if you see the Light honey make sure
> it don't make you blind if you wanna bite
> the apple make sure the apple don't bite
> you back all musicians are looking
> back looking back looking back to see
> if love has followed them home

I put my pen down and hold my left hand
like a newborn baby the doctor put me on
antidepressants and sedatives but I stopped taking
them after a week or two I drink instead
I am a trapped tiger I pour myself another drink
I hold it up to the gloomy light from the window
the ice makes its own music

there was this flamenco dancer I used to see
when I was a child I wanted her rhythm I wanted
to be that rhythm I wanted to be her

I drink my drink she tried to teach me
but I was just too clumsy that's the smallest I ever
felt and so I stuck to my piano and kept her mad steps
in my fingers I finish my drink

I go to the piano my left-hand twitches to life
like that dancer I start to play the keys
no that's not right the keys begin to play me
I am the instrument and the piano is the musician

I remember being 20 years old and hearing
on the radio that the Russians sent a dog into space
I felt so sad for that dog what was her name?
is she still up there? does she want company?
her name is jumping and panting
on the tip of my tongue

I want to keep my left hand
I want to keep my irony intact
I want to dance
with Laika Laika Laika

RABID

These days when I try to nap
I hear something out there in the maze
of the city backscatter lurking
through dead of winter

I hate the sound so I get dressed and I go out
and trap it like the rodent it is I breathe in
the fevers the steam gets stuck between fingers
my head is swimming with glowing fish
it's an underwater city

and under the eyes of Neptune
I must look lost drifting down the cobblestones
a wretched cigarette hanging out of my lips
a furrowed brow keeping me warm

I remember what you said that late night
over bad coffee the night we got stuck
to each other

        don't you know honey the worst thing
        that can ever happen is nothing?

I turn a corner
I see the plaza where people are getting in
and out of taxi cabs everyone's jitterbugging
but it's all a farce isn't it? the children play
with a table they place a soda bottle at one end
of the table and hit the table at the other end
to make the bottle pop up in the air

they do it to pass the time they can't wait
to grow into their regrets

I was the wormhole swirling invisibly
in the middle of your galaxy sucking everything in
even time itself you'd spent your whole life
avoiding me the suck working through you

I was the reason the moon came apart
in your sky I was a rabid dog spiraling
closer and closer I have grown so cold
when I pick up an apple and bite into it

my bite disappears
and the apple is whole again

HIDDEN MOUNTAIN

What idiocy!
the cabin is north
and what is north
anyway?

the cabin is a speck in the evergreen sea
and I could miss it by fifty miles hell three hundred

I entrust my life to a little magnetized needle
what idiocy! and what is true north when the truth
is an ongoing negotiation? the only certainty
is I am going to die

such hubris to think I could walk away
from everything make myself as scarce
as a good magic act

the woods have swallowed me up
and all the creatures will converge upon me
take me apart slowly and deliberately
and I will feel every fang and tongue fighting
for my heart tearing and pulling
this is what the woods do

lead me to the light behind the pain
I continue north the mountain appears in mist
profound in her stillness terrible in her beauty
two roads meet at the peak

this idiot reaches out to her
because everything she holds is true
particularly her silence

54

THE MOON CANNOT BE STOLEN

Four o'clock in the morning I have too much wine
in my belly when I manage it I sleep on benches
kicking out my legs against my will I wake up now
and then and read newspapers left behind

in one article I read of an opera singer
who lost her million-dollar voice
in the middle of a performance

        composed shot of her manager
        careful shot of crowds beneath her balcony
        candles holding tears

I walk around the station for an hour
I buy a coffee and try to pretend I've slept the night
this makes me stone-like the sun rises
through the windows like a blood snot

I'm not going to make it a thousand stars fading
I ask for one I might fit in my pocket
with all its holes

I walk those last two blocks to my hotel
head upstairs and slide naked under the covers
I simply wait for her knock at the door
or her phone call whichever cuts the haze

across the dark table of sleep ten crows fly
in a circle the sky turns yellow three clouds pass
by phone rings the psychic invites me to her party
I ask for directions and she tells me to follow the water

I walk through the wind pass some skateboarders
giving me stink-eye

I reach the psychic's castle where she offers me
wine and pills and I take it all in swells of laughter
then we sit at the dining table the lights are out
our eyes are closed we are lost in the spirit world
unhinged open to all the songs of heaven and hell
we unfold and bloom with cathedral-sized wishes

      the world must burn she whispers it's a song
      they sing it goes somewhere strange
      you've been there before you've been there
      before

her eyes opaque the psychic takes my hand leads
me down the hallway to her room the snow returns
the heat stays on we talk about seeing Ulaanbaatar
together I help her make sangria chopping fruit
and making a mess as the guests tumble in

some producer approaches me and starts talking
with this smile like a dentist sits next to him prepared
to remove anything caught in this mouth full of razors

      do you remember me?
      he asks

yes I say I remember you from a night several years
ago I remember you I couldn't read your mind I
couldn't tell where you were going with your words
I remember you even in your kindness there was a
cold wind blowing through you your tongue was a
greasy eel you were certain every secret wasted

56

the heart

        that was me he says
        you were going to send me a treatment
        what happened?

he introduces his film between sips of sangria
we have no choice we are a captive audience
he pushes the buttons turns the dials
lowers the lights

a van pulls down the gravel path the robbers
pace the motel room The Driver in shirt and
tie potbelly sticking out flicking on and off
the light switch The Brain is at the table counting
the cash The Muscle's eating corn on the cob
they make small talk then go their separate ways
the film degrades the story falls apart in sex
and ennui a signal we should all do the same

the shootout comes applause
a bit too much if you ask me
(what are we protecting?)
but then we'd survived made it through
the wastes and wilds our invisible hands
grasping at the reeds and rushes fade out

when I go take a piss a lightning bug flutters
all about the toilet the producer is standing
outside when I leave and I don't tell him
about the bug it's a secret my own thoughts
my own space in this tiny world and if I tell him

about the bug then we'd only be walking
up and down broken escalators for the rest
of the evening there'd be no beginning and no end
just mouths running all night long

Ulaanbaatar is gone the psychic mutters in my ear
lost somewhere in the storms lost somewhere
in those singing throats Ulaanbaatar is gone
she says lost in the runoff lost up a cheerleader's skirt
lost in the baffles of God across The City of Blue Skies
runs flesh the sun swindled into life
and we'll never catch it

we talk into the wee hours the sirens come and go
the party ends in sign language I am on the streets
the snow falling in cuts and bruises the moon
a fuzzy speck I pull my skull cap down over my ears
cross the road zigzag through some morning fools
each arguing over the definition of fascism
I forget myself in a cigarette

the sky barks as three clouds pass overhead
the snow sneaks under my scarf no time no rest
nothing but the news and the curve of the Earth
in each footstep a grip and a breath of glass

I count my steps palms blanched violets swirling
in my guts the sky barks and I bark in imitation
no lies no melodies no whispers no fingerprints
odd creatures tread the foam dancing outside
the moonlight the rhythm in my elbows yes
the story is born there with waves and lights
repeating a city stretched thin sputters and sparks
we'll dance and sing

there is no message but a sigh carried
across the still ocean I feel the psychic's strength
inside my blood it conquers me turns me
inside out I am that sigh I am that pair of hands
crowning me I am the child wiping away the tears
standing up speaking let us do our ghostly work
ice fashioned by flame I speak to you I have no one
I speak to you
I get a different room in a different hotel
under a different name it's a small room
but the bed is nice and big I figure I'll sleep
for a few hours I look out the window and see
the moon she flashes her tattoo
a private viewing

after a shower I crawl into bed and scream
into my pillow until sleep comes heavy

CON JOB

The kid ran up to me holding out
his broken glasses and working the tears
and his friends said I'd bumped into him
as I rode by on my board back at the corner
and how was he supposed to see now?
and his winter coat had a rip in it
along the shoulder which someone had patched
with masking tape

and I could see the act was an act
but it was something real too so I said
gee sorry and I went on with my day
because the whole bee-stung world says no
and no and no until it's yesyesyes
and we're all of us trying to keep
from The Great Dog of Hell

VILLAIN

A piano crashes strings are flailing keys
and hammers and dampers bouncing wild
on asphalt

all in perfect silence and then a conspiracy
of voices fools and idiots I can only make out
a few words here and there they go on

and on forever an echo of an echo of an echo
and I operate from a darkened room

with a full-length mirror across the way
and maybe a window or a door and if I could see
only one color it would be the gold in an owl's eye
the piano crashes and I fall

into the dark and the man with the half-face comes
to me whispers in my ear and tells me what to do
just drivels on and on this half-faced clown

there must be something else going on I think
there must be music playing somewhere
the piano crashes and I sleep for six thousand years

some creeping urge overwhelms me my senses
coalesce into something resembling a soul
I am absent until voices begin to form faces

with memories attached behind the eyes
something is moving there in the voices too
it takes a long time for that soul that person
that face to come

into focus and then he's here and here he is

peek-a-boo

his face palsied on one side he's found
my hiding place tunneled his way in his voice
like cracked bells at midnight his eyes dead

he says it has always come to this
my loverly

there's a rumbling in the guts
something is forcing itself out of my mouth
a locust it keeps trying to fly out
and it is screaming and I keep my ears open

time clacks along and the faces start to turn
to masks I want to be here I want to be here
now and now and now but no one hears me
I am looking back at the scene of the accident
the shadows will cover it sometime soon
and I tell myself that much is certain

the half-faced man comes for me
when the moon fades

the problem with curiosity
he says
is you lose yourself and become

the curious thing a new guest coming up
the steps with flowers

I can see the piano crashing black wood revealing
its pale grain the soundboard shooting sparks
into the morning the lid flapping against emptiness

an echo of an echo of an echo yes there's music
playing somewhere the circle opens just a crack
and the universe rushes in I was someone

once upon a time but now I'm more or less
of an idea of someone and so I protect you now
in the dark ask the moon at midnight his scent
like fresh concrete

it has always come to this
my loverly

TWO CATS

It's an old house the roof caved in
a garbage lid about to be taken away by the wind
and there is a storm coming but it's slow
and sustained a rash of doldrums inside the house

everything is covered in cobwebs and mouse-shit
and graffiti and empty beer cans and liquor bottles
this is a place where time is moving backwards
and sidewards we know such places exist
because it is not such an unreasonable thought

like when you are on a train
and for a second you don't know if you're moving
or the train next to you is moving

two cats come back to this old house now and then
they like to walk across the piano walk their odd
music whenever they do this they inevitably
conjure ghosts

first the father appears in his suspenders
his can of Budweiser in one hand
and his Camel cigarette in the other hand
he speaks without moving his mouth
but it's quite easy to hear him since his voice
rattles every nail in the house

> Green in yea house he maketh life me paths
> leadeth

he rambles on and on he's chock full of proverbs
but they're all scrambled eggs

when he's done thumping
he gets down to business

> I'm suffocating they want me to wear a mask
> over my mask over my mask over my mask
> over my

he quiets down after a while the cats grow bored
of his melody so they sing the mother's melody

her melody is true even with the strings
so out of tune she comes in a rush of gossamer
a rush of sighs

> father does not dream he is a butterfly
> but he walks out into the night
> onto a shining city on a hill
> with black helicopters floating
> welcome welcome he is drooling
> over prisms trapped in engine oil
> in the jargon of astronomy
> the eyes starved red and chthonic
> creeping out of their sockets he makes
> his way to work and the phone is ringing
> and he walks from one cubicle to the next
> following the ringing as it leaps from lilypad
> to lilypad he has to pick it up the economy
> in his wrists the faith in his knees there's
> nothing else but those ringing gods and
> meanwhile I ride the pale green horse
> through moonless night

the two cats say goodbye to their mother
she disperses into the air the cats jump off
the piano slowly they are both getting on
in their years

ca-thunk ca-thunk

they hope to see mother again soon
but they are in no rush the woods
are still full enough of wonder

they make their way into this warm
summer night full up with silk and silence

SPASM

It takes me out to sea I can't fake
my way out of the maelstrom I can't refuse

it takes me in its hands picks me up and turns
me upside down and the sand falls
out of the top of my head

I get up there's nothing in my pockets to find
but lint and follow the white lights the glitter
of my failures in the asphalt—I fly into the sky

playing that same old record no one's to blame
this time gravity holds no sound the streets full
and fuller with water a flood of indecision

pain don't be anything not the weeping deer
nor silver surfer in the end we're just two thieves
standing in the rain

NEW YEAR'S KISS

start this party w/o me the wrong people
are drunk and I think I smoked opium
but I'm not sure I want entirely out
of this foolishness

someone's calling my name on the streets
someone's got something new to heal me
pass these flickering streetlights
and wander into the dark find myself
a vein of gold take the hot dose start my engines
in the afterglow

there's a couple kissing in the new year

does anybody know
who invented the kiss?
how could it be somebody
who'd never kissed?

be careful with joy
when nary a thing is left out of place
you just might be okay

MATADOR

O the bulls are restless for my blood horns twitch
in the bullring out of the dark the dark flies out

don't let those angry angels pull me to the ground
better step back Jack these bulls light up forget

the details like who lit the match and who spilled
the gas here he comes for your candy-cane ass

a bird's eye view of your troubled soul as murder
falls on art and money and all the times I pretended

to care this darkness was not made for kids like us
the ones who carry sun into sun our mothers' wish

for us to survive just one more night touch the sky
touch the stars with our fingertips and olé olé

RAW

Reflect upon the sushi chef who watched
the slow and deadening traffic on the drag
from 2:30 till 4:30 those cocktail hour stretches

reflect upon his little window tangled branches
allowing the grey clouds to peek faint shadows
passersby pulled out of shape he gauged
their faces he sneered at some when they took
the time to look waved at others when they met
his face at 5:00 he chopped flesh and rolled
tuna whitefish salmon the greatest hits
an endless creation resurrection a blurring
of hands screaming in silence each to know
but he is as dead as all the soft flesh he cut
unmade unraveled nothing left of him but salt
and curses alas he made the job of being human
too goddamn easy surely he'd die a better death
than this the gnashing teeth of the wild dogs
of sepsis here's wishing ol' Mama Death will hold
him in her arms and give him warmth
and he'll drink her milk

but what was it he used to say about wishes?
oh yeah wish in one hand and shit in the other
and see which one fills first

reflect muse deliberate upon the sushi chef
who watched the streets explode contract
and the ladies wear their sun hats from 2:30
to 4:30 those cocktail hours stretches

ROOMMATES

The wind and rain weave in the snow
sculpting a maze in which to lose my wits

without this maze I won't hear you whistling
from one room to another asking someone
to fill in the blanks shore up the defenses

without this maze I won't hear your melody
float from one room to another while I stare
into dark spots on the snow

without this maze I am sitting high up
a wall come join me nothing closer to heaven
come join me

OVERKILL

700 years I danced on broken glass I danced
and sang tossing wine into a starless sky
but I never wrote to let you hear my echoes

700 years I danced on shattered mirrors scars
accumulated in the soles my sanctity lost
but ever closer to my name flashing
like passing trains in a mess of rails
if only I'd written to see if you moved
past metaphor

700 years I danced and sang alone strangled
by God asking after the fluttering in the garden
the beast crowning in the dawn
but I never asked after your soul

700 years I asked questions & 700 silences
returned I belong to you now your planets
and their satellites

700 years is over in the blink of an eye
but it's your eye to behold

700 years I toiled and fretted I danced
on shards of glass I sang because I had rhythm
the quiet to lead me to you my new name
in the palm of your hand

AMERICA

There's a raven hanging around my box
he sticks around and talks to me tall trees
sway in the night

he says I shouldn't talk back to him
because I am not crazy a raven cannot speak
a raven cannot tell me anything I don't know

and I don't know where the raven goes
when the sun sinks—to his tall trees in the night
perhaps I don't care for I am no longer lost

I have found my home I've come a long way
to get here to the tower working and working
to keep us alive I live close to the tower
in my box

the tower asks us to tell stories so we tell stories
tell the tower what we know we send our words
into the night shapes we make in the dark

the tower hears everything and can you hear it
whirring and clacking? a tower so tall it reaches
into the pink clouds the women and children safe

inside the tower they feed inside the tower
the women and children are safe inside no longer
out in the wilderness I don't know

what I am without the tower without my guiding
light the calculations are done in there when done
the drums dole out the winner's name

we stand around in our tattered clothes and wait
only the tower can make us pure again inside
the machines are at work the machines never stop

working on their calculations to prevent the drifting
of souls the machines tell us how and what to think
how to act react how to worship dutifully

see us gathering around the tower and listening
to the hums of the machines inside—an itch
in its circuits won't go away look at us

our sunburned faces waiting for the tower to glow
and radiate again we are returning to the foot
of the tower at dusk and dawn to hear the gears

cranks and bells a prelude to the drums
I hope it is me this time I will stand on top
of the tower with a machine gun the women

and children will be released I will fire
into the heart of the crowd men women children
I kiss them with bullets some panic & run some stand

at attention some shit themselves they will worship
me for a day and a night then the tower will know
me and I will know the tower and the women

& children will feed on the dead tall trees sway
in the night the raven tells me and if
you shut off the machines inside you'd all vanish

can you spy me up high now? the raven says
I play your protector I protect you from you
come on and let me soothe you with the songs

draw a circle around you draw a circle
in the biting sand of night and stand inside it
don't worry you will be perfectly safe inside
an automatic prayer

bit by bit you eat you've come a long way
bit by bit you worship the tower your kind arrive
at an unprecedented rate we will always be here

in this arrangement there will always be a machine
and there will always be love you wait for the killer
to be chosen you praise the day when the killer fires

into the crowd into the heart of everyone no greater
blessing than a kiss from a bullet

WOMB

Out of the black the surf swirled in my ears
rhythms riding through the grey saltwater
filled my mouth reached for my throat
grasped for my heart life

commanded my lungs to spew out an arc
of bile and ocean I searched through the fog
my ear picked up a whisper of bird call
I tried to stand up slipped

and fell the rough grain of the ground
scoured my palms a ground both rough
and slippery I thought it should be sand
beneath me the surf

receded I saw what I thought was driftwood
as I crawled forward the surf pushed
from behind leading me smack into iron bars
when it rushed out

again I grabbed the bars I saw my hands worn
knuckles and scars no reflection played
on the water so I couldn't see my face
the waves came again

I peered through the fog but I couldn't see
beyond the surf's reach I gripped
each bar tightly moving from one to the next

until I came to a corner the surf hit me
on my right side as I turned I reached a door
and tried to open it I ran my fingers

up and down the door and discovered

the pawn-shaped keyhole no scream came out
but I screamed out anyway a bird called out
you pointed your spear at my heart your eyes
were full of fear enhanced by the red and white
war paint running across your face you screamed

your voice breaking through the surf you backed
away from me slowly no don't leave me I said
but I could barely hear my own voice you turned

and ran into the fog I fell again to the floor
of the cage the waves moved back and forth
over me

night came and the tide was rising I was going
to drown the waves broke over the top
and I was underwater about to take my first breath

of ocean something jabbed at my head
from above it was a reed a hollow reed I breathed
through it and when the tide lowered in the morning
I saw you

standing on top of the cage
with the reed in your hands

you did this every night helped me to breathe
you brought me food through the cage for years
and years until the bars rusted
and I was free

NOTHING DOING

Dark figure approaching from across a field
speckled with lightning bugs something
to its stride its slender legs and arms
like a fresh scarecrow

so this is what you look like nothing much
just your average phantom I expected to see
more details as you drew closer but you remain
a blur might as well give you a name how 'bout
Mr. Nothing Doing?

come closer closer stand right in front of me
no not there there hmm no real face there
only the mist of stones and a licorice breath
still your cartoon eyes cut through the murk

it was you provided the tears and screams
the treasures that cursed our hearts
the constellations of grief in the cloak of night
the space in between the well of fevers
where twilight sparkled all faces reflected

you've given away everything to frighten us
but it only made us kiss the walls in thanks kiss
with our feet barely touching the grass we floated
a hundred years except for you

Mr. Nothing Doing

all those nights you held yourself a dying dog
with the moon your only witness
where is your everything?

I can hear your teeth chattering fearing my voice
in this expanse I can see a meteor threatening
to rip the sky wide open

I'm glad you have no heart because it means more
room for my own and it is excellent news
your eyes are so close together what else can they see
but me?

alas I've given you nothing sir and you've returned
the favor with grace Mr. Nothing Doing holding
hands is all that's left so take my hand
what's it matter in the end? a dream persists
against the dark lightning bug or bonfire
no matter we float in clouds and land
upon a roof from here we can see the horizon
and more to the point the horizon can see us

I lose grip of you and you lose hold of me
and my bullshit no matter ghosts and numbness
et cetera et cetera Calliope comes anyway
she knows the score

STRANGE CITIES

Fresh snow rocks and streams
covered in white trees with limbs
begging the sky empty field safe
under a blanket of ice the air slows
silence retreating into itself
the opposite of an echo building
inward like a snail for sleep
there's some order to it:
each flake has a place
and time to fall the world
of ten thousand things disappears
what remains belongs
the river flows impossibly
—and the silence will be enough
flakes falling on flakes in the void
of trees two eagles fight over a worm

follow the river wending my way
through a blind landscape towards
distant spires making ripples in the sky
I let the river lead me
to this strange city the river twists
and the sky doesn't fall the city folk
wave to each other they are wishing
they could be everywhere at once
I can teach them how will they
recognize me? for I am all things
and nothing ah to reach Avalon

I must be invisible

a beast cries out a Thing discovers itself
inside and out a testament to Becoming
from the shadows of the woods the snow
has not reached the forest floor the footfalls
crunch less and less in a soft and giving soil
the cries are louder my ears twitch
there comes the metallic scent of blood
tearing into fresh kill ripping tendon
and muscle exposing what nature opts
to hide the gleaming pluck—or else
it's a matter of prescience

the quarry
is me I am the dreamer after all
one foot in front
of the other toward the cries

the moon is watching me the elements
will not decrease move air move water move fire
move earth to force resurrection
whatever takes me to the strange cities
on the hills

AN AMERICAN TRIPS

This is happening this is going to hurt
I am locked into a trajectory of pain
I won't attempt to fall gracefully
this is happening
I should've looked where I was going
why did I think it was two steps instead
of three?

gravity is doing its work now the sky is above me
and the ground is beneath me will my insurance
cover the cosmetic surgery for my nose?

this is me half asleep in my snarkolepsy
somewhere in between hiding and seeking
only one thing could lure me out now
a blue heron listening to my heart

in the wilds in the shadows of the city in broad
daylight I know I thought it was just two more
steps but it was three perhaps I should've been
paying attention this is happening

I'm drunk on apocalypse drunk on my own
research drunk on hate on God gas prices hope
for the future true crime novels fast food
and bullets chasing Christ through the corn

maybe that's why I'm losing my balance
I mean I've been acting weird lately
like the raging idiot at a party who knows a little
bit about everything but nothing about anything
certainly nothing to save his soul

when I was a kid dreaming about plump
girls dancing under orange trees I said
I knew I didn't know anything remember
the river swelling beneath the moon?

after you help me up and dust me off
will I dream it all up again?
will fresh new ideas spring
from my recent fall from grace?

or will I let everyone live?
at least before my lawyers arrive?

the blue heron's standing in the cool mists
of summer this is happening here's a cartoon
star for when I meet the marble steps

yes you know me better than I know myself
I am the agent provocateur the carnival barker
seeking the fire inside the fruit my balance
is where I last left it down the thousand garden

paths down where the demon dreams
down where sweet kisses do not relent
down in paradise with the snake and the apple
and the knowledge I don't need to live there

to keep my balance Eve did me a huge favor
when she bit the apple all those years ago
so why am I still falling all the time?

I'll stop crying get up
dust myself off this time
and keep climbing
I decide what is at the top
of these marble steps
if you want my opinion
we could use a library

CLOUDS

There's a man walking in the clouds
walking across the sky his suit is nice
he's nice everything is nice as knives
there's a man walking in the clouds
above the Atlantic

the cars are all dead the roads are choked
everyone's disappeared but me and him
we're walking in the moonbeams walking
in the mist walking in no direction

the sea rages in its house a billion prayers
tossed in spray

FAWN

She's cracked & broken up
the grass won't cover up her remains
scattered innocent the bug-filled rain
gets draped across the fen my eyes
& dying takes a lifetime to declare

I saw her laying behind the abandoned
church her trembling legs those ears
their twitching game her eyes obsidian
I should've kept my wits
searched for dry wood trees above her
swaying wild another storm another
chance to float beneath the waving clouds

the lightning came and saw her glint
and a bolt descended loud & proud
the birds took off into the blossom dark
I ran to her and she was lit within I picked her
up a moon she was a moon afloat
in concentration

the moon is safe we die into the bones
of earth the marrow of consciousness
o bones of earth
shall she become the rain again? we live
to die we die to live & in my arms
she turned into the moon O bones
of earth O bones

MIRROR

If I know myself if I know myself
inside the mirror I'll know myself
I'll know myself if I kiss you on the ear
if I kiss you on the ear will you whisper
come back home to me if I dream of love
does love receive the dreaming
and the rain? I was born inside the heart
and in the bowels of the earth
I was born inside the heart stealing
the heart I can't remember or forget
I'm crying like a doctor tell me no lies
I want you to know my face is blue
I want you to know the storm's been raging
all night long while you investigated fear
hoping for a change where I live
it's in my head no one gets hurt
should you find yourself here better hide
my love does not reach the sky
pretty please carry me into the sky
ain't it funny when you know what you are?
you belong in this dream just remember
there are no headlines in death no jungle
of fangs no scandal of sickness

let us traffic in hope it is not beyond us or
beneath us is this everything? the faint drums
and the lightning

Andrew Condouris is a writer and an English teacher in
Trenton Public Schools. He graduated from Fairleigh
Dickinson University's MFA program. Andrew has
published online and in print in various literary magazines.
This is his first published collection of poems.

Made in United States
North Haven, CT
27 February 2024

49291788R00055